Animal Babies

Do the Strangest Things

· Written & Illustrated by Charles Fuge ·

MoonDance

Baby ducks will follow
the first thing that they see . . .

. . . whether it's their mother

or a baby chimpanzee.

Platypuses are not birds.
But look! They hatch from eggs.

Little baby frogs and toads have tails, not arms and legs.

Baby Asian elephants
are **fuzzy when they're born.**

And, at first, a baby rhino only has a tiny horn.

Little baby black bears
feel safest up a tree.
Meerkat babies aren't afraid
of snakes, as you can see.

Daddy sea horse has the babies,
without any fuss.

A baby humpback whale
is as heavy as a bus.

A baby emperor penguin
nests upon his daddy's feet.

A baby seal is white as snow
to match the white ice sheet.

Look out! Here comes a tiny train
made out of baby shrews.
Watching from Mother's pouch
is best for baby kangaroos.

Koala babies ride upright,
upon their mommies' backs.

But upside down's the right way up
for baby sloths and bats.

Baby moths and butterflies

look nothing like their mothers . . .

. . . and baby tigers play fight
with their sisters and their brothers.

Alligator babies
ride safe in Mother's jaws.
And little baby boys and girls
like crawling on all fours.